A Gift For:

SWEETS

From:

NUGGET

Editor: Lindsay Evans
Art Director: Chris Opheim
Designer: Rob Latimer
Production Designer: Bryan Ring

ISBN: 978-1-59530-516-9
BOK1208

Printed and bound in China
OCT12

true Love

By Melvina Young

Hallmark
gift books

YOU'RE SUCH A BIG PART of my Life.

The good part.

you're my heart's safe place
in the world...

my best friend,
my Love.

if a gorgeous movie star showed up at the door with wine and flowers...

I'D take the wine
and flowers
and wait for you
to get here.

even when you're not right here
so that i can lean into you...

you hold me up
with your strength.

I Love you and, miraculously,
you Love me back.

Mess-ups,
fall-downs,
fails, and all.

we could start a fire.

no matches
necessary.

you make me want
to kiss more slowly,
hold on more tightly,
believe more passionately,
and give more completely.

You make me want
to Love you
more and more.

$$(you) + (me)^2 = \text{happiness (forever)}$$

JUST DOING *THE* math.

together we've made
our own little world
where we never
have to worry about
being someone we're not
or some way we're not.

I love

being

"US"

together.

YOU WATCH MOVIES

YOU DON'T EVEN LIKE

JUST BECAUSE I DO.

Now that's
Love.

we feLL IN Love BY cHANce.

I start to Laugh
and you pick it up
Like you're finishing
one of my sentences.

I love that about us.

you fill up my empty spaces.

I feel completely
complete
with you.

we work just as hard
at Liking each other
as we do
at Loving each other.

We're

muLtitaskers

like that.

our Love isn't always a fairy tale, but it's a pretty good story.

And it's
JUST
OURS.

we DON'T HAVE to waIt
foR tHe SUN to set peRfectLy
OR tHe staRs to LIGHt
tHe NIGHt sky JUSt RIGHt.

We know
how beautiful
what we have

IS.

OUR LOVE CAN BE messy sometimes.

But it
cleans up
pretty
nice!

we do "hot and steamy"

but our
"nice and easy"
is just as good.

"*I Love you.*"
smaLL, simpLe worDs.
Big, Beautiful feeLings.

SO HAPPY
WE'RE
SHARING
THEM.

you've got a hold on me —
heart and soul,
body and mind,
totally and completely.

Love doesn't have to be perfect.

it just

has to be

strong.

Like ours.

what you give me — incredible.

HOW I LOVE YOU FOR IT — ENTIRELY.

anyone who doesn't believe
that Love can save the world...

has never been loved by you.

we can't argue with Love.

Occasionally
with each other.
BUT NEVER
WITH OUR LOVE.

my hand in yours,
your heart with mine...

perfect fit.

the heart.

it's just a muscle really.

How it performs this thing called *"Love"* — *that's the miracle.*

I WOULD totaLLy
be "waRD anD JuNe"
witH you.

Actually, I'd even be

"HOMER AND MARGE"

with you.

As long as it's *WITH YOU.*

I found someone
who knows me,
accepts me, and
understands me
in exactly
the way i need...

the day
that I
found you.

that beat my heart skipped...

that was you dancing your way into it.

we can do Love
in all the ways we want,
in every way we need...

plus in some ways
we haven't even
imagined yet.

ocean deep
mountain high
galaxy big

my Love
for you

you came into my Life and Loved me so
deeply and so right...

I knew
I could tie
my lifeline
to yours.

forever going into eternity...

that's

how long

i plan

on loving

you.

if scientists knew how much better
our Love makes *everything*...

they'd *DEFINITELY* want to clone us.

we're so hot together.

The sun has *got* to be jealous!

"forever" is a Long time.

Just not
long enough
to be
with you.

you've seen
"first thing in the morning" me
and decided
i'm still pretty lovable.

How could I not
Love you
even more
for that?

a Love Like ours couLd never
be an accident of fate
or a trick of chance.

you're my destiny.

HOLDING ON. NEVER LETTING GO.

For us,

it's that simple.

know what i'm
Looking forward to with you?

Love with a Little silver around the edges,
a few character Lines on its face,
and more substance at its heart.

we're just going to get better with time.

tHe way yoU Love me
makes It so easy to Love yoU...

with everything in me

we can laugh at the small stuff
and get through the big things.

That's why
we'll always
be good
together.

OUR STORY BEGAN
WITH A SOUL-DEEP "I LOVE YOU"
AND THE SWEETEST KIND OF KISS.

It could only end with
"forever and ever."

Love Lasts...

past sweet kisses
and nervous laughter,
through intense passion
and calm friendship,
through happy times
and moments that try us.
our Love Lasts.

OUR LOVE DREAMS BIG,
takes CHANCES,
Leaps WITHOUT fear...

and lands in beautiful places
we never thought possible.

i'm already so deeply in love with you.

SO HOW COME
I feeL LIke
I HAVE
SO MUCH
FURTHER
to faLL?

if you have enjoyed this book
or it has spoken to your Love in some way,
we would Love to hear from you.

Please send your comments to:
Hallmark Book Feedback
P.O. Box 419034
Mail Drop 215
Kansas City, MO 64141

Or e-mail us at:
booknotes@hallmark.com